Original title:
Quantum Quandaries

Copyright © 2025 Creative Arts Management OÜ
All rights reserved.

Author: Nora Sinclair
ISBN HARDBACK: 978-1-80567-786-4
ISBN PAPERBACK: 978-1-80567-907-3

Uncertainty's Embrace

In a world where cats can hide,
We ponder where the quirks abide.
Schrodinger's pet, both here and gone,
Laughing at our midnight con.

A particle that waves hello,
Decides to spin, then twirl, then go.
Confusion reigns, but what a show,
We giggle while the doubts bestow.

To measure or not, that's the game,
The outcome's wild, but who's to blame?
When every answer leads to more,
Our minds are like a wobbly door.

So hold tight to your cosmic joke,
A universe that loves to poke.
In this dance of strange delight,
Even the math seems to take flight.

Fractured Realities

Two worlds collide in a playful fight,
One's rather dark, the other's bright.
With every glance, a scene may swap,
In laughter's grasp, we cannot stop.

Through a lens that bends and twists,
We chase the shadows, and something missed.
Reality's joke, a complex jest,
Who knows which version's truly best?

As particles laugh at our dismay,
They play a game of hide and sway.
We'll join their fun, as we explore,
The silly truth of what's in store.

So grab your friend and take a ride,
On this wild wave of what might bide.
In fractured tales of nights and days,
We'll find the joy in strange displays.

The Dance of Particles

A waltz of bits in unseen space,
They jiggle, jig, and change their pace.
Sometimes they're here, then off they flit,
A cosmic ball, our minds admit.

Their twirls are not of grand ballet,
But hop and skip in their own way.
With every move, they tease our minds,
In jester's garb, the truth unwinds.

A photon shimmies, can't stay put,
While neutrinos play their game of foot.
In this grand jig, the laughter's bright,
As bosons boogie through the night.

So when you ponder tiny things,
And question where a giggle clings,
Just dance along the physics flow,
And let your silly spirit show.

Schrödinger's Shadow

What's in the box? A friend or foe?
In clever tales, the answer's low.
Tails of cats and clever tricks,
In shadowy realms where planck time ticks.

We joke and jest behind closed doors,
As curious minds tumble and implore.
Is it a cat or just a schmo?
We hold our breath for the grand show.

In every paradox, there's a twist,
A wink of fate that can't be missed.
We chase the shadows, up and down,
In Schrödinger's world, we wear a crown.

So let's embrace the silly strain,
In every quandary, joy will reign.
For laughter hides in every crease,
In shadows deep, we find our peace.

The Infinite Reflection

In a mirror that laughs, it shows my face,
But I look like a raccoon in a funny race.
It winks back at me with a comical blink,
I ponder if mirrors also need to think.

Reflections can chatter, they giggle and glow,
With each flicker and shuffle, they put on a show.
Oh, to dive deep in that whimsical land,
Where every glance leaves me feeling quite grand!

Orbits of Otherness

An asteroid plays hide and seek with the stars,
While planets enjoy racing in comical cars.
They swirl around laughter, in loops they all spin,
Making jokes 'bout the gravity, how can they win?

Comets crack jokes as they zoom by in haste,
While moons wink at Earth in an orbital chase.
In this cosmic ballet, funny quirks abound,
In a universe vast, silliness is found!

Ephemeral Eternities

Time tickles itself in a clock that's absurd,
It whispers sweet nothings, oh haven't you heard?
Each second's a jester, a prankster in line,
With minutes that dance like they've had too much wine.

An hourglass giggles, sand slips with delight,
Its grains doing cha-chas, in broad daylight.
What's fleeting feels endless in this curious game,
Where laughs echo 'eternal' and never feel lame!

The Riddle of Reality

What's real, what's a mirage, what's pizza for sure?
I ponder the puzzle, and laugh at the lure.
To think of a world where cats wear cute hats,
And logic just lays down while dancing with rats.

A riddle of questions that tickle the mind,
As answers keep running off, leaving me kind.
In this raucous reality, full of surprise,
I giggle at wonders framed in funny ties!

Shadows of the Future

In a world where cats can talk,
And shadows dance around the clock,
I asked a ghost for his advice,
He offered me a cup of rice.

Time machines made of cardboard,
With buttons marked by a bored lord,
I pressed one and the dog turned blue,
Now he thinks he's a kangaroo.

Shadows in Superposition

There's a cat on the roof who's sleeping,
In two states, it's just leaping,
Am I dreaming or is it real?
Maybe both? That's quite the deal!

Tangled up in a ball of yarn,
Decisions made without a plan;
Each choice exists in the same space,
Until I find the right embrace.

Dimensions of Desire

I wrote a note to my future self,
It ended up on the bookshelf,
In a world where socks have feelings,
They waltz around with comic reelings.

In parallel worlds where pizzas fly,
I chased one, thinking it'd comply;
But every bite is just a dream,
It seems my pizza's lost its steam.

Chaotic Harmonies

In an orchestra of sneezes,
A symphony of cheese pleases;
The conductor's a squirrel with flair,
Who insists on playing in mid-air.

Dancing notes from the out of tune,
With rhythms set on a broomstick moon;
As I join in, my feet go wild,
And the cat watches, bemused and mild.

Fractures in Reality

In a world where cats can fly,
The toaster dreams of pie in the sky.
But when you look, it's just a lie,
Reality wobbles, oh me, oh my!

A squirrel chats with stars at night,
While shadows dance in frantic flight.
Gravity simply lost the fight,
And chairs decide to flee in fright!

Superpositioned Secrets

Here I am, both late and on time,
Eating toast, but it feels like crime.
Waves and particles in a rhyme,
This breakfast choice can't be a climb.

In the fridge lies a ghostly slice,
Is it fresh? It looks quite nice.
Now it's here, now it's not, so precise,
Superpose the ketchup with some spice!

The Curious Case of Entanglement

A pair of socks that won't behave,
One's lost, and the universe waves.
It's tangled up, like I might shave,
But I can't find the other brave!

Two peas in a pod, that's what they say,
Yet one rolled off in a cheeky way.
Entangled tales that make me sway,
Where did my sense of style decay?

Schrödinger's Dilemma

In a box that holds my lunch, oh dear,
Is it safe or has it turned to fear?
A sandwich waits, though it's unclear,
Is this gourmet or foul frontier?

A cat inside the box might grin,
Do I dare peek or just dive in?
The odds of lunch are wearing thin,
But I'll flip that coin with a cheeky grin!

The Paradoxical Pulse

In a world where cats are kings,
Chasing shadows, oh what fun it brings.
The dog thinks it's a solar flare,
But really it's just fluff and air.

Jumping particles in a race,
One's in this place, another in space.
They giggle at our puzzled gaze,
As we try to count their quirky ways.

Time tickles as it bends and warps,
Like a clown juggling generational torps.
We might just be a ripple's prank,
Floating in a cosmic tank.

So let's dance under the weirdest beams,
In this funny realm of fractured dreams.
Where laughter echoes through the void,
And logic's a game still un-deployed.

Etched in Energy

Electrons laugh in whirlwinds tight,
Doing the cha-cha, out of sight.
While photons sip tea with a grin,
Discussing how to make a spin.

Here lies the doodle of a cosmic jest,
As forces play tag; they never rest.
Each blink and twist becomes a joke,
In the circus where notions poke.

Waves crash in a playful glance,
While particles line up to dance.
A jester's hat atop a star,
Silly cosmos, you've come so far.

So let's giggle at this dizzy show,
As everything bounces to and fro.
In energy's art, we take our stand,
And giggle like kids in a wonderland.

Flickers of Existence

In this tunnel of light and glee,
A flicker says, 'I'm happy to be!'
Existence plays hide-and-seek,
While photons brush up on the unique.

Wormholes tickle the fabric tight,
Pulling us into a funny fright.
We giggle as we tumble through,
Stumbling upon a cosmic stew.

Everything's swirling in a jest,
Atoms making jokes, doing their best.
Reality gives a mischievous wink,
Dancing in a nebula of pink.

So let's frolic where the waves collide,
In a realm where giggles never hide.
Flickers here shine bright and bold,
As we revel in wonders untold.

Beyond the Horizon of Thought

Beneath thoughts that sail afar,
Ideas sprout like a curious star.
Blending laughter with a sprinkle of glee,
As we ponder what's wild and free.

In the corners of the mental maze,
Absurdity reigns in playful ways.
Thoughts waltz through the silly and grand,
Building castles made of sand.

We giggle as reason takes a back seat,
To ponder the riddles—so bittersweet.
Three drinks of logic and a splash of jest,
In the land where nonsense is the best.

So leap beyond those boundaries tight,
Crack a smile, chase after light.
For in the chaos, we might just find,
The zany gifts of a wandering mind.

The Illusion of Time

Tick-tock goes the clock, looks so sly,
Yet time is a trickster, oh my my!
Yesterday's news, today's déjà vu,
Got coffee in hand, but what should I do?

A second feels long, but a year flies by,
I swear I just blinked, caught a nap, oh why?
Chasing the hour, I trip on my shoes,
Should I check my watch, or just take a snooze?

Cycles of Collapse

Round and round, the orbits spin,
Falling flat, that's how we begin.
Gravity pulls, yet up we go,
Like a cat on a roof, putting on a show!

Chaos dances in loops and swirls,
Making a mess, oh those tricky curls.
Like socks in the dryer, lost in the fray,
Every spin leaves me dismayed anyway!

The Nature of Being

I sit and I ponder, am I just a wave?
Caught in a cycle, trying to behave.
What is my purpose? A laugh or a frown?
Eating my pancakes, wearing my crown.

Who knew existence could be such a lark?
Like a cat with a laser, chasing a spark.
Fleeting moments, they come and they go,
Like my leftover fries—where did they go?

Unraveled Mysteries

Tangled in thoughts that make no sense,
Like trying to pet a cat on the fence.
With riddles aplenty and puzzles galore,
I'm left scratching my head, always wanting more.

I opened my mind, it fell out with a thud,
Brain in a pickle, it's stuck in the mud.
The answers are hiding, oh where could they be?
Maybe in the couch… or under a tree?

The Vibrations of Void

In the silence, molecules play,
Tickling strings in a quirky way.
Atoms dance, a comical sight,
Fluctuating in the dead of night.

A vacuum hums, like a kazoo,
Invisible laughter, who knew?
Particles prance, in random glee,
Waving to none, just like me.

Empty space has a lively groove,
It wobbles and jiggles—watch it move!
Gravity's got jokes, it sways and bends,
Pretends to be serious, but it pretends.

In the void where no one can see,
Silly chaos plays hide and seek.
If space can giggle, then so can we,
In this cosmic joke, just let it be!

Duality's Perspective

A wave and a particle walk into a bar,
One's all fluid, the other's bizarre.
They argue and jest in a merry debate,
"Am I you, or are you great?"

Light confesses, "I've got both sides!"
While the particles nod, and take their rides.
Bouncing between two frames so fine,
In this dance of duality, let's sip some wine.

Schrodinger's cat, it's both here and not,
Playing hide and seek with some cosmic plot.
Is it alive, well, or just on a spree?
This feline's confusion tickles me!

In the realm where opposites collide,
Both ends of the spectrum take a ride.
Laughing at logic, they cheer and sway,
In this whimsical world, let's laugh away!

Cosmic Coincidences

Stars align in a comical mess,
As fate juggles its cosmic guess.
A planet slips on a moonlit truck,
Saying, "Oops! That's just my luck!"

Comets sneezing with tails so bright,
"Excuse me, just passing through tonight!"
Galaxies swirl in a giggly race,
Gravitating towards a cosmic embrace.

A black hole trips on its own dark mist,
Not even the light can exit its fist.
It laughs, "I've swallowed too much this time,"
While the universe chuckles, oh so sublime.

So toss your wishes to the cosmic stew,
With a wink from the stars, and a giggle too.
For when chance takes a twist, do not despair,
The universe gifts humor beyond compare!

Fragments of a Cosmic Puzzle

Scattered pieces float through space,
Like confetti from a wild race.
Stars whisper secrets, bits and bobs,
In a cosmic jigsaw, scatter and sobs.

Galaxies twirl, a puzzling dance,
Each piece a mystery, if given a chance.
Nebulae swirl like a painter's splatter,
Creating a canvas, where bits can chatter.

One corner's a planet, another a sun,
In this puzzling light, we all can have fun.
Connect the dots with a giggle and wink,
In the vastness of space, we share and think.

So don't fret if your piece seems amiss,
In this cosmic puzzle, we all find bliss.
With laughter and joy, let's fit them in,
For the universe smiles when we begin!

The Dance of Probability

In a world where chances twirl,
Dancing dice give fate a whirl.
Flip a coin, heads or tails,
In this game, no one prevails.

A cat is both here and not,
In a box, it ties a knot.
Jumps from sleepy to alive,
In this chaos, we all thrive.

Every choice a wild cha-cha,
Life's a joke, we laugh ha-ha!
Spin the wheel, what will it land?
Surely luck is not so planned!

Yet we twirl with joy and cheer,
In this realm, nothing is clear.
We prance and leap like it's a dream,
In this dance, we all redeem.

Particles in Paradox

Little specks that bounce and tease,
A game of hide-and-seek with ease.
Sometimes a wave, sometimes a dot,
What they are? Well, that's the plot.

One foot here and one foot there,
They travel fast, but don't you stare.
Caught in knots of cosmic play,
On their antics, we spin away.

Two particles in a tight embrace,
Entangled woes, an endless chase.
Do they argue? Do they jest?
In their antics, we invest.

From particles that race and spin,
To quirky tales, we all dive in.
In this paradoxical spree,
We laugh at fate's absurdity.

Shadows of Uncertainty

Ghostly forms that tease the light,
In the dark, they dance with fright.
Fickle shadows, what's your game?
Hide and seek, none are the same.

Poking fun at what we seek,
In the quiet, they all sneak.
Are they here, or are they gone?
In this riddle, we all yawn.

One fleeting thought, then another,
Joking with both friend and brother.
Cloaked in mystery and in jest,
Shadows swirl, they never rest.

In the depths of this delight,
We find laughter late at night.
As uncertainty takes the stage,
We smile bright and turn the page.

The Wave-Function Waltz

Twirl and dip, it's quite the scene,
A waltz of chance, you know what I mean.
Probability, sliding by,
As we reach for the endless sky.

One moment here, the next, who knows?
In this ballroom, chaos flows.
With every step, can you be sure?
Or is this dance just an allure?

Frequencies hum, they twist and shout,
Dancing particles, they flit about.
On this floor, life's a grand charade,
Where certainty is simply delayed.

So let us dance, give fate a spin,
In this waltz, we let joy win.
Laughing with every twist and turn,
In this rhythm, there's so much to learn.

Light's Mysterious Path

In a world where photons play,
They dance and twinkle night and day.
They hide in corners, peek around,
Leaving us all in laughter bound.

A beam of light just had a joke,
It traveled fast, then gave a poke.
"What's the rate for bending space?"
"Oh, it's quite cheap, just follow pace!"

In tunnels where the shadows gleam,
Light bounces back, a cosmic dream.
It giggles softly, makes us grin,
While particles spin and twist within.

So, if you chase a ray of fun,
Remember, dear, it's never done.
For light is tricky, oh so sly,
It hides where laughter dares to fly.

Echoes Across the Multiverse

In realms where echoes laugh and shout,
Dimensions swirl, there's no doubt.
A twinkle here, a ripple there,
It's chaos wrapped in cosmic flair.

In one world, cats are kings in hats,
While dogs analyze the secret stats.
What would Einstein think of this?
"Just another universe, nothing amiss!"

A giggle escaped a cosmic void,
As spacetime's fabric got overjoyed.
"Hey, did you hear the one I told?"
"No, tell me quick, my friend is bold!"

Across the multiverse, they share a laugh,
An atom's whisper, a cosmic gaffe.
As paths collide and humor strikes,
The universe winks, living on bike!

The Silent Symphony of Atoms

Atoms gather, what a show,
They dance in silence, with a glow.
"What's that sound?" a neutron kids,
"Just vibrations of our playful bids!"

Protons hum a jovial tune,
While electrons boogie round the moon.
"Let's form a band, it's time to jam!"
"With bass from quarks, I am the slam!"

In this microscopic dance of cheer,
A symphony only we can hear.
Each bond a stitch in fabric tight,
An orchestra lost in pure delight.

But wait! What's that? A hiccup near?
An atom burped, oh what a sphere!
With laughter loud, they play their part,
In the grand rhythm of the heart.

Labyrinths of Light

In mazes where the photons race,
They zigzag here, they spin with grace.
"Where to next in this twisty plight?"
"Just follow the laughter, it feels just right!"

Mirrors giggle, bending beams,
Creating echoes of wild dreams.
A lightbulb flickers, "I know the way!"
"Let's turn on the fun, come what may!"

In these corridors of dazzling glee,
Light plays tricks, then winks at me.
"Can you keep up, or will you drown?"
"Just point me to the nearest town!"

Through circuits, loops, and dazzling bends,
Light finds paths where laughter blends.
So take a step in this merry maze,
And let the spark ignite your days!

Collapsing Dreams

In a world where cats can fly,
And cows demand a pie,
Dreams collapse like marbles,
Rolling off the table.

Llamas wearing sunglasses,
Discussing life with buzzes,
Is it real or just a snag?
Pull the thread, watch it drag.

Pigeons in a poker game,
Bluffing with no hint of shame,
A folding chair, a funny stance,
Who knew they loved to dance?

In this circus of the mind,
Lucky charms are hard to find,
Tangled thoughts, a wild spree,
Welcome to my comedy!

The Clockwork of Chaos

Tick-tock, the clock might sigh,
As spaghetti falls from the sky,
Ninjas on skateboards zoom,
Creating chaos in the room.

The toaster's now a DJ,
Spinning toast in cheesy sway,
While fish wear tiny hats,
Debating politics with sprats.

A penguin in a bowtie,
Serves tea with a gleeful eye,
Who needs order in this haze?
Let's dance through the quirky maze.

Time loops like a rubber band,
In this wacky wonderland,
Forget the path, let's just prance,
And take a moment to dance!

Hidden Dimensions

Behind the wall, a cat appears,
Wearing glasses, sipping beers,
He claims to know the secret ways,
To navigate the bizarre maze.

Bubbles float in velvet green,
Spilling secrets yet unseen,
Rabbits pull from hats their knives,
Telling tales of other lives.

In pockets deep, my thoughts reside,
In twisty paths they like to hide,
Where socks are friends, and chairs can talk,
And spaces dance in tilted walk.

What if you were just a dream?
Caught within a wild scheme?
Let's giggle softly at our fate,
And appreciate the odd debate.

Flickering Realities

In a world where muffins speak,
And shadows play hide and seek,
Glitches swap the day for night,
As noodles glow with neon light.

A cow with wings goes mooing loud,
As robotic frogs attract the crowd,
Jumping high, they laugh and cheer,
Making Mondays disappear.

Fish in suits hold boardroom talks,
Arguing over quantum clocks,
While bananas rocket through the air,
Creating joy with every flair.

Twist and turn, we spin around,
Where laughter's always to be found,
In flickering truths and jolly sights,
Embrace the funny in our flights.

The Science of Surreal

In the realm where cats can dance,
And mice may wear a pair of pants,
The laws of physics take a twist,
As squirrels plot and coffee's missed.

A wormhole leads to lunch today,
Where sandwiches swim and dolphins play.
Time loops back for one more pie,
And gravity's a silly lie.

Mirrors show you what you crave,
A cupcake that can ride a wave.
The test tubes cheer with glee and zest,
In this lab where chaos loves the best.

So grab a hat and dance around,
With sparkly thoughts that know no bound.
In science's grip, we lose our fears,
As laughter rings through space and years.

Quantum Reflections

A universe of pizza slices,
Where toppings scheme with several vices,
Twirling quarks and floating cheese,
All dance to rhythms, with grace and ease.

Reflections bounce like rubber balls,
Through tiny doors and funky halls,
A cat appears and then he's gone,
Sipping tea on a unicorn lawn.

Doppelgängers play hide and seek,
One laughs aloud while others speak,
Reality's a jester's game,
Where logic wears a silly name.

So let's embrace the whimsy's call,
And leap through chaos, heed the sprawl,
With every laugh, a world takes flight,
In realms of giggles, pure delight.

Recipes for Reality

Mix a tablespoon of bright ideas,
With a sprinkle of cosmic cheers,
Stir in a dash of silly space,
And you'll soon find a smiling face.

Add a pinch of playful lies,
Like flying frogs or rainbow skies,
Simmer in a pot of dreams,
Where laughter bubbles, gleeful streams.

Pour it out on plates of stars,
And serve with sides of candy bars,
Each bite transforms a frown to glee,
In this dish, the mind runs free.

So cook with whimsy, let love spread,
In every slice of pumpkin bread,
The secret's out, it's fun, you see,
In every recipe, reality.

The Spaces Between

In the silence where the thought-bugs play,
And whispers dance in the light of day,
There's a riddle that hides in plain sight,
Tickling ears with joy and delight.

The pauses hold the funniest things,
Like rubber ducks with tiny wings,
In every gap, a laughter blooms,
As echoes chase away the glooms.

Between the stars and winks of fate,
A hamster dreams at an open gate,
Leaping through the void with finesse,
In spaces where quirks start to impress.

So tune your heart to the gaps in sound,
Where silly thoughts are tightly wound,
In the spaces where we misplace,
A spark of joy we all can embrace.

Infinite Intricacies

In a box of cats, time does twist,
A wink from one, by chance you missed.
They leap through loops, like jelly beans,
Wobbling time, in chaotic scenes.

A toast to the odd with a fizzy cheer,
The mouse is here, but it's not quite clear.
On a string of thoughts, we dance and play,
Through worlds where logic's gone astray.

Here comes a quark, wearing a hat,
Saying hello to a talking bat.
With every giggle, the cosmos spins,
In this zany whirl, where fun begins.

The puzzle grows brighter, flips like a page,
As laughter erupts from the cosmic stage.
With absurdity thick, like warm apple pie,
We ponder the strange, all while we fly.

Split Infinity

Two paths diverge at a fork in time,
One leads to reason, the other to rhyme.
A squirrel in a suit offers advice,
But which version's fun, oh that's the spice!

The paradox giggles, tickles the air,
With all of existence, it doesn't care.
Take a step left, or perhaps the right,
The universe chuckles, it's quite the sight.

With each new choice, the cosmos sways,
As cats and dogs dance in quantum plays.
Confusing the rules is part of the fun,
When every decision means you've won!

Snap your fingers, and there's the twist,
Life's not a math test; it's a playful list.
Embrace the weird, let chaos ensue,
And find joy in the oddness dancing in you.

Curious Cat Conundrum

A cat in a box, oh what a stretch,
Is it alive, or just a fetch?
With a wink and a yawn, it ponders a clue,
In a universe where none can subdue.

It chases a laser that's clever and bright,
But is it just photons, or pure delight?
With every jump, it defies all the odds,
While pondering mysteries that baffle the gods.

Under the sofa, it hides and observes,
The nature of time, oh how it swerves!
The clock ticks backward, the fridge hums a tune,
It dances with shadows, under the moon.

In this feline frolic, there's laughter in gloom,
As paradox kitties bring life to the room.
So let's join the circus, with tails held high,
In a world full of quirks, we'll never say die!

The Measure of Dreams

In the dreamscape, where nonsense reigns,
A ruler's misplaced, it's burst at the seams.
With clocks that melt, and unicorns on trains,
We measure the giggles, the wildest of themes.

A hurry to dream, so sleep's not a waste,
Where numbers do pirouettes, and grapes play bass.
Let's sip on the whimsy, a flamboyant taste,
As the dance of the bizarre takes us to space.

With mathematical cats clad in polka dots,
Throwing confetti as laughter erupts.
In this crazy world where sanity rots,
We'll capture the jest, and our madness corrupts.

So here's to the moments both silly and odd,
Where dreams take shape, and we all stand awed.
Here's the measure of fun, it's a rosy façade,
In a universe wide, that's perpetually flawed.

A Glimpse Beyond the Veil

In a realm where particles dance and play,
Bouncing off walls in a curious way.
A cat in a box, still pondering fate,
Is it alive? Oh wait, that's just great!

Photons flit by, they can barely be seen,
Like shy little sprites, oh so keen.
They giggle and sparkle, in beams of bright light,
As scientists chuckle, 'Is this wrong or right?'

Entangled connections, they twist and they weave,
A cosmic joke, oh you wouldn't believe!
A wink from the cosmos, all tangled we are,
With particles joking from near and afar.

So peek 'neath the veil, get ready to smile,
For science is funny, in its own quirky style.
With riddles and puzzles, it leads us to jest,
In this vast universe, we're all just a guest!

Entropy's Embrace

In a world of chaos, it's hard to find peace,
Where socks disappear and mess seems to increase.
Entropy giggles, tossing rules to the breeze,
It's like a wild party, that'll never cease!

A cup spills coffee, just look at the fun,
The floor's now a canvas, where chaos has won.
As order surrenders to entropy's reign,
We've got a new pet: a dust bunny named Lane!

The universe whispers, 'Embrace the dismay!'
'We'll dance on the rubble, come what may!'
So here's to the disorder, we cheer in delight,
For embracing the chaos makes everything bright!

So if your life seems a tangled old thread,
Just laugh and enjoy it, then follow instead.
For in this wild dance, we may just understand,
That life's sweetest moments are drawn in the sand!

Whispers of the Invisible

In silence they flutter, the tiny unseen,
Invisible forces all slink in between.
With scientific whispers, they're making their rounds,
These cheeky small critters in silence abound.

Gravity chuckles, a pull here and there,
It tugs on your feet, like it's not even fair.
While magnets flirt fiercely with a tiny 'zing',
A romantic duet, with a twist in the swing!

The air is a riddle, can you feel it? No way!
Yet it lifts up our voices, so we can all play.
So smile at the void, the hidden delight,
For the whispers of physics are charmingly bright.

As we ponder the unseen, a giggle breaks through,
For in every mystery, there's fun to pursue.
So lift your glass high, to the things you can't see,
For life's full of laughter, let it all be free!

The Fabric of Nothingness

In a tapestry woven with threads of pure air,
Nothing whispers softly like it doesn't care.
Yet in every blank space, potential does bloom,
Perhaps it's just waiting to leap from the gloom.

But wait, what is nothing? A tricky old chap,
It's hiding in corners, setting a trap.
A magician doing a vanishing act,
Just when you find it, it's nowhere intact!

Particles pop in like clowns at a show,
One moment they're here, then they're off with a bow.
So nothing becomes something, a puzzling delight,
A comedy sketch under dim candlelight.

So let's toast to nothing, so full of surprise,
With laughs from the cosmos, and stars in our eyes.
For in this grand theater, the absurd is the key,
To relishing life's antics, wild and free!

Subatomic Silhouettes

In the realm of tiny bits,
Particles dance and do their skits,
A quark skips by, a gluon twirls,
Creating chaos in the curls.

Photons race, they hold the light,
But can't decide if day or night,
A neutron snickers, neutrinos drift,
In this strange world, they give a lift.

An atom whispers, "Watch me glow!"
While electrons spin, putting on a show,
Do they have secrets, or just a laugh?
Let's split a joke, then split a half!

So here we ponder, in never-ending space,
Subatomic silhouettes, in lively race,
They wink and giggle, oh what a spree,
In this mad dance, we all agree.

Whims of the Universe

Oh how the cosmos loves to tease,
With things that jiggle, wobble, and freeze,
Stars play hide and seek with fate,
Bending rules, it's never late.

Planets spin in comedic style,
Comets whizz and smile a while,
Black holes sigh, then quickly munch,
While asteroids gather for a crunchy lunch.

Galaxies swirl in a dizzy waltz,
Mysteries rise, but no one faults,
Gravity's joke pulls us all close,
A cosmic party, we love the most!

With laughter echoing across the sky,
The universe chuckles, you can't deny,
In these whims of space and time,
Finding joy in the cosmic rhyme.

The Mirage of Measurable

In a world where math can't quite agree,
Numbers vanish like a bumblebee,
The measure of fun is hard to find,
Like counting sand grains, it plays with your mind.

The length of a joke is truly bizarre,
Stretch it too long, it won't go far,
And yet laughter's the ruler, so grand,
In this laughter, we take a stand.

Scales tip and jiggle when we're having fun,
Who needs a gauge when we're spun?
A humorous riddle is our common ground,
In mirages of laughter, true joy is found.

So let's toss out rules, for a wonderful spree,
Even in chaos, we can agree,
The funny path is where we'll trod,
In the mirage of life, we'll find our nod.

Cosmic Choreographies

Stars in a ballet, spinning divine,
Dancing around like they own the line,
Nebulas twirl in colors so bright,
While supernovae put on a fright!

Galaxies glide in an elegant sweep,
While solar flares do a flip, and leap,
Asteroids tap dance with their cohort,
In this cosmic show, we have a sport.

Planets slide with a graceful flair,
In the ballroom of space, floating in air,
A pirouette here, a jet there,
In this cosmic choreography, we all care.

So let's give a cheer for the stellar crew,
In the universe's dance, there's space for you,
With every pirouette, and every glide,
We laugh and we twirl on this cosmic ride.

Cosmic Dilemmas

In a universe that's quite absurd,
Particles dance without a word.
Gravity's pulling my socks askew,
While Schrödinger's cat just snoozes too.

Aliens claim they're flying high,
But they just stopped for a piece of pie.
Wormholes bend time like a swirly straw,
I forgot my keys—ain't that the law?

Entangled Thoughts

Two ideas tangled in a flurry,
Both are right, without a hurry.
One says coffee, the other tea,
Confusion brews infinitely!

Thoughts bubble like a fizzy drink,
In a cosmic sink, I start to think.
Quantum leap to the fridge so near,
But I trip on space—oh dear, oh dear!

The Paradox of Possibilities

In a box I sit with endless chance,
Maybe I'll leap or maybe I'll dance.
Infinite paths ahead with glee,
Yet I choose to just watch TV.

A paradox wearing mismatched socks,
Could this be what the cosmos knocks?
With every choice, the universe grins,
While my laundry pile quietly spins.

Waves and Whispers

Waves whisper secrets, rippling through space,
They tickle the stars in a playful race.
My toaster pops, making breakfast cheer,
As the universe giggles—can you hear?

Interference patterns mess up my hair,
Like those tangled thoughts that float in the air.
On a surfboard of stardust, I ride and glide,
In the cosmic playground, let's take a ride!

The Nature of Illusion

In boxes where cats both sleep and play,
A wave and a particle dance in ballet.
They blink and they vanish, oh what a sight,
Is it daydream or nightmare? Let's ponder tonight.

A photon appears, then it's gone in a blink,
It teases our senses, then smiles with a wink.
You find it in light, or perhaps in the dark,
But don't ask too much, or it'll make its mark!

We chase after shadows, but they lead us astray,
How many are needed for a quantum bouquet?
One, two, or more? It's a comical game,
With laughter and fumbles, we vie for a name.

So here's to the mystery, let's raise a cheer,
For quirks of the cosmos, we hold dear.
We'll laugh at the chaos, the folly we see,
In our dance with existence — oh, quirky and free!

Riddles of Resonance

In a world where the rules seem totally bent,
We laugh at the echoes, their strange discontent.
Like a joke that unravels with every new twist,
Just keep on giggling, you get the gist!

Particles spin in a dizzying whirl,
A dance of confusion, a quantum girl.
With every question, a chuckle ensues,
Like a jester in court, it's hard to refuse.

They say opposites attract with glee,
Like socks in the dryer, just let them be free.
When they meet in the middle, oh what a surprise,
A riddle unspooled, before our own eyes!

So let's toast to the laughter, the games we cannot see,
In riddles and rhymes, we find jubilee.
So join in the fun, and let's not take a bow,
For the universe chuckles, right here and right now!

Threads of Existence

A string that connects us, or pulls us apart,
In a web made of laughter, we each play our part.
With a wink and a nod, we slide down the line,
Confused, amused, in this fabric divine.

Tangled and knotted, we tangle some more,
Like jigsaw puzzles stuck behind a locked door.
Do you pull on the thread, or just let it be?
In this tapestry wild, is there space for a bee?

We're woven together through giggles and sighs,
Each moment a stitch in this wacky disguise.
With laughter like yarn, it can tangle and flow,
So let's knit up some joy, and let all the fun grow!

In threads of existence, we find our delight,
With a chuckle and cheer, we will dance through the night.
So come grab a skein, let's make something grand,
In the loom of the cosmos, together we stand!

The Enigma of Existence

In a universe strange, where logic takes flight,
We ponder and joke on the edge of the night.
A paradox wrapped in a riddle's embrace,
Like a cat in a box, just humor in space.

Questions arise like popcorn that pops,
Where do we go when the answer just flops?
Is it here, or it's there, or maybe it's both?
With a grin and a giggle, we're sworn to an oath.

We chase after answers that shimmy and sway,
Like trying to catch shadows at the end of the day.
With whimsy as our guide and laughter our muse,
Existence is funny, with comedic views!

So here's to the mysteries that tickle our brains,
And the joy in the puzzles, the laughter that reigns.
In the enigma of life, let's dance hand in hand,
With humor as our beacon, so blissfully planned!

Igniting the Invisible

A cat in a box, it purrs and it yawns,
While Schrödinger laughs at his famous brawns.
The lightbulbs flicker, a dance of delight,
As photons take turns, switching left and right.

A cup of hot tea, it's both there and not,
My breakfast is toast, or maybe just rot.
The universe chuckles, a cosmic jest,
In the kitchen of fate, we're all but a guest.

The toaster can toast, or perhaps it won't,
A dilemma quite rich, or just a bad font.
Is this sandwich alive? Will it jump off the plate?
The fridge hums a tune, like a strange blind date.

So let's raise a glass, to the things we can't see,
Where laughter's the answer, is that just me?
We tap the absurd, in the glow of a spark,
In the glow of the unseen, let's make our mark.

Worlds Within Worlds

In a world filled with socks, lost in the wash,
Are they hiding with keys, in a strange little posh?
The universe giggles, it has quite the stash,
Of particles dancing, in a quantum-like bash.

A saucer spins well, but does it even care?
Do galaxies waltz in the zero-grav air?
With twisty old noodles, the cosmos holds court,
While planets play poker, in a pie-chart sport.

A ball bounces back, or does it leap away?
In probabilities tangled, we laugh and we play.
With quarks in a hurry, and leptons on break,
Each tick of the clock feels like a big fake.

So here's to the riddles, and mysteries grand,
In bubbles of thought, we all take a stand.
May the giggles be loud, as we ponder the primes,
In worlds ever shifting, with delightful rhymes.

The Shimmer of Uncertainty

Like ducks on a pond, with a hint of a quack,
Do they float or sink? Now that's quite the hack.
The ripples are laughing, a merry old game,
In a state of suspense, nothing's ever the same.

A coin flip's a dance, heads or tails will win,
Who knew such a toss could unleash such a spin?
With bets on the table, the crowd starts to cheer,
As uncertainty whispers, 'I'm always right here.'

Do aliens cheer when the planets align?
Or just sit there with snacks, sharing some wine?
In the vastness of space, humor often appears,
With the stars sharing jokes, through the laughter and tears.

So fizz up your quirks, let them bubble and pop,
In the shimmer of chaos, we laugh till we drop.
For life's just a puzzle, with pieces that jest,
Unraveling hilarity is surely the best.

Reality in Flux

In a universe, wibbly and bent,
Cats in boxes, oh, what a event!
Particles dance with a giggly glee,
Where's my sandwich? I can't even see!

To be, or not—that's the big trick,
Like finding a penny that looks really slick.
Reality bends like a rubbery toy,
I'm lost in a maze that's just full of joy.

Collapsing waves and jokes on repeat,
Every measurement tastes like a treat.
Observer's eye gives a mischievous wink,
Silly physics makes us rethink!

In this strange realm where the oddball thrives,
Laughing at nature as it dives and dives.
With quips and quirks, we refuse to conform,
In laughter's embrace, we humorously swarm!

Fabric of Whimsy

Threads of chaos weave through the air,
Stitching together a cosmic fair.
Tangled in fabric, we spin and we sway,
Where socks disappear—who knows, hoooray?

Buttons of matter, they jiggle and pop,
While twirling around, they never do stop.
Knots of serendipity, all in a line,
A riddle so funny, it's simply divine.

Patching a quilt from the stars above,
Stitched with the laughter of those that we love.
In playful patterns, we've found our delight,
As whimsy wraps us, so light and so bright.

With each odd twist, we grin ear to ear,
Life's a funny game, let's give a cheer.
In the fabric of wonder, we dance without fear,
Together we laugh, all woes disappear!

Schrödinger's Smile

In a box where uncertainty blooms,
A feline juggles both doom and tunes.
Is it happy, or is it sad?
Both states are fun, isn't that rad?

With a whisker twitch, each secret unfolds,
In a world where probability holds.
Fluffy purrs or a ghostly howl,
Makes debating a serious growl!

Superpositions, like socks in a load,
Where mischief reigns, and logic's on road.
Do we peek, or just let it be?
A great big chuckle pinned under the tree!

As we ponder, we can't help but grin,
Life's just a game that's a little akin.
In every paradox, we find our style,
Embrace the unknown with Schrödinger's smile!

Entropy's Muse

In the dance of chaos, there's joy to be found,
As order takes flight and spins all around.
Each moment tumbling, a whimsical feat,
Entropic ballet on a wayward street.

With time as our partner, we glide and we twist,
A jumbled jigsaw, a humorous mist.
Lost socks and spilled drinks create a delight,
As entropy chuckles throughout the night.

Messy is pretty; oh, join in the fun,
With whirls of confusion, we've only begun.
In disorder's embrace, we discover the game,
As giggles erupt and we all feel the same.

So toast to the chaos, the grand masquerade,
In entropy's arms, we gleefully wade.
Let laughter cascade, let smiles be the muse,
In the wild and the messy, there's nothing to lose!

Unseen Forces at Play

A particle dances, spins in the air,
While I just sit here, in my old chair.
What makes it twirl? Is it a hidden prank?
Or do they just like to mess with my flank?

In the lab, we poke and prod with delight,
While electrons giggle, avoiding our sight.
They play hide and seek, with a mischievous grin,
Oh, how I wish I could join in their spin!

A photon flickers, just a flash in the dark,
With clever intentions, it shoots like a spark.
I ask my cat, "Do you see what I mean?"
It just licks its paw, clearly bored of the scene.

So here I am, lost in a cosmic jest,
While mystery particles put my mind to rest.
The laughter of physics, it echoes so sly,
As I ponder the forces that tick and defy.

Realms Beyond Reason

In a land where logic takes a vacation,
We frolic with thoughts of wild creation.
A cat in a box, what a curious case,
With fuzzy friends lounging in Schrödinger's space.

The universe giggles, defying our norms,
As gravity winks in its own playful forms.
Who needs a compass when chaos delights?
Let's chase all the riddles the cosmos ignites!

In fractal trees where the numbers don't end,
Each branch tells a joke from an unseen friend.
Let's dance with the glitches, embrace the absurd,
For in realms beyond reason, the fun is preferred!

So gather your thoughts, like lost little socks,
And join in the lunacy, twist time like a fox.
Embrace all the puzzles, let laughter impart,
In the silly domain where we play with the heart.

The Mystique of Motion

A speedster spins and bends through the light,
With a wink, it travels, oh what a sight!
And here I am, feeling so slow and frail,
Wishing I could ride on its wild, twirly trail.

Objects in motion, they quirk and they sway,
Like they're on a stage, putting on a play.
I try to join in, but I trip on my shoes,
While particles whirl like they've got nothing to lose.

As things zip and zoom, I scratch my own head,
Do they write the script, or am I misled?
With laughter resounding in every quick turn,
I ponder this dance that makes my brain churn.

So let's toast to the jiggle and wiggle of life,
To all the odd motions that slice through our strife.
For in this grand ballet, though I stumble and fall,
The mystique of motion makes me smile most of all.

Timeless Awakenings

In a clockless realm where seconds don't tick,
I find that all clocks just play hide-and-seek.
The past is a prankster, teasing with tales,
While the future's a riddle that giggles and fails.

Each moment's elastic, it stretches and twirls,
Like a jester who trips, causing giggles and whirls.
I ask my reflection, "What time is this, friend?"
It chuckles back softly, "It's all just pretend!"

The past is a kitten with nine little lives,
And the future's a pie that's still waiting for pies.
In this loop of absurdity, I'm free and unbound,
While the universe jests, spinning time all around.

So let's frolic with seconds and dance through the now,
In realms of forever, let's figure out how.
For in timeless awakenings, laughter will bloom,
As we float through the cosmos beyond all the gloom.

Out of the Particle Fog

In a lab, particles dance and twirl,
Electrons giggle, giving it a swirl.
Photons wink like mischievous sprites,
Can't trust them, they're tricky little lights.

Protons puff out, with a grandiose stance,
While neutrons just sit, lost in their trance.
Quarks play hide and seek, loud with glee,
Bumping into each other, like kids at a spree.

When measured, they jump, oh what a surprise,
Never quite ready to show their disguise.
Clocks tick awkwardly; toast seems so far,
In this particle fog, we can't be a star.

Mirror of Many Worlds

In one world, I'm a hero, saving the day,
In another, I've burnt all the toast I won't pay.
Cats rule the chaos, and dogs write the songs,
In my mirror, right's often wrong with new throngs.

I ask, "Is that really me on the wall?"
With a wink and a nod, it gives me a call.
Parallel shapes of bad puns abound,
Where laughter echoes and joy knows no bound.

In one world, I dance dressed as a tomato,
In another, I'm wise, like a cosmic potato.
Peeking through glass, oh what do I see?
Just layers of options, of choices - whee!

Nucleus of the Unknown

Deep in the middle of all that we know,
Lives a nucleus, putting on quite a show.
Hiding in its shell, it whispers a tune,
"Come join the chaos, let's dance to the moon!"

Oh, protons are prancing, no reason or sense,
While neutrons mutter, feeling quite dense.
Electrons are spinning, a dizzying spree,
"Who left the door open? Come play, come see!"

Like a party gone wild, with snacks all around,
A nucleus' heartbeat is a curious sound.
Mysteries linger, they giggle and tease,
In this atomic hub, it's all just a breeze.

Temporal Tangles

Time takes a tangle, it twists and it bends,
Like spaghetti on plates, right at the ends.
Tick tock, it giggles, then trips on a dime,
Flipping through moments, both silly and prime.

Looping around like a ouroboros kite,
Where cats chase their tails, oh, what a delight!
Futures collide with the past so odd,
In this twisted timeline, I take a quick nod.

"Is it breakfast or dinner?" I ponder in jest,
With clocks spinning wildly; they just need some rest.
Time's like a rubber band, stretched and then snapped,
In this comical tangle, we all feel quite strapped.

A Voyage Through the Void

In a realm where cats can fly,
And fish wear hats, oh my!
Where time's a stretchy, silly thing,
And clocks just laugh and sing.

The toaster talks with witty jests,
While socks play chess, they're the best!
In this void where logic bends,
Each twist and turn, a giggle sends.

A ship of thoughts, it sails so bright,
Through mismatched stars in the night.
What's down is up; what's up is down,
We float on giggles, not a frown.

So let's embark on this wild quest,
With quirks and quirks, we're truly blessed.
In this absurdity, we'll dance and prance,
Oh, what a fun, bewildering chance!

Horizons of Hypothesis

In fields where theories tumble down,
And rabbits wear a scholar's gown.
Where paradoxes ride on bikes,
And logic often takes long hikes.

The sun flips pancakes, gold and crisp,
While space debates with a comic wisp.
With options branching, all askew,
The mind wanders; what's real? Who knew?

Floating thoughts in jelly pots,
Wobbling on the edge of knots.
Each question leads to more delight,
Where entropy can spark a fight.

So let's explore this whacky land,
With giggles shared and ideas grand.
In the maze of thought, we'll chase the fun,
Creating chaos, every one!

Breaches of the Known

In realms where rules just seem to hide,
And ducks pretend they're bona fide.
Where gravity has lost its shoes,
And logic always sings the blues.

The laws of nature take a break,
As gummy worms begin to quake.
Who needs a map when you can fly?
Let's flip the script and give it a try!

Sandwiches dance on the kitchen floor,
While cupcakes plot a cosmic war.
Reality's twisty, what a sight!
As laughter echoes through the night.

Let's tumble down this rabbit hole,
With munchies stacked and hearts on a roll.
In funny tales where truth is skewed,
We'll find the joy in all that's brewed!

The Canvas of Chaos

With colors splashed in wild array,
And bubbles that just love to sway.
The canvas quakes with painter's whim,
As cats in bowties sing a hymn.

Splotches giggle, consciousness sings,
While robots dance on rubber springs.
With each brushstroke, the world can spin,
Oh, watch the chaos dive right in!

Clouds of candy swirl around,
As logic takes a merry round.
In this art, we lose the frown,
And tumble into colors' crown.

So splash and dash, let's make a mess,
In the chaos, we'll find our zest.
With laughter high and spirits bold,
A funny tale for all retold!

Disentangling Dreams

In a world where cats can fly,
I questioned why the sun is shy.
A toast to socks that lose their pair,
And unicorns who take up air.

A bean can dance, a spoon can sing,
Just wait to see what the toaster brings!
With jellybeans that twirl and sway,
Who knew chaos could be such play?

The moon sings songs of jumbled fate,
As gravity just celebrates.
A giggle here, a chuckle there,
In this topsy-turvy affair.

So as we chase elusive dreams,
Just remember, nothing's as it seems.
With laughter echoing in our hearts,
The universe thrives on funny arts.

The Halo of the Horizon

On the edge where the sky meets sea,
Wobbly waves just laugh with glee.
A light bulb floats like a feather,
As seagulls argue over weather.

A rubber duck in a cosmic race,
Zooming through outer space!
Planets wear their silliest hats,
Beware of sneezing mutant cats!

The sun did trip on its own beam,
Creating shadows that giggle and scream.
A comet that forgot to glide,
Is trapped in a game of cosmic slide.

Watch out for the horizon's grin,
It knows all the silly tricks within.
With every dull and serious sigh,
It sparkles, laughs, and says goodbye.

Perplexities of Particle Play

Tiny bits of matter dance,
In a most peculiar prance.
Atoms whisper secrets old,
While electrons flash like gold.

A neutron bows, a proton spins,
Creating laughter where it begins.
Why do particles giggle, you'd ask?
They've mastered the art of a clever mask!

With every bounce, a joke unfolds,
A chuckle from the quarks retold.
They roll around like kids at play,
In a universe that's far from gray.

So when the chaos seems too much,
Remember particles love to touch.
Their goofy games light up the night,
Turning confusion into pure delight.

Quantum Whispers

Beneath the stars where secrets hum,
Whispers of the cosmos drum.
A squirrel in a spacey hat,
Sipping tea with a funky cat.

It twirls and spins like a dizzy thought,
Lost in the puzzles science wrought.
Time runs backward, or so they say,
While socks escape in a merry play.

A riddle in the air, so absurd,
Chasing whispers, beautifully blurred.
Einstein laughs in his own way,
As reasoning takes its humorous sway.

In the grand scheme of cosmic fun,
What's serious can easily shun.
So let's unwind, become untied,
In a universe where giggles abide.

www.ingramcontent.com/pod-product-compliance
Lightning Source LLC
Chambersburg PA
CBHW071844160426
43209CB00003B/401